Discovering Ballet

The houselights are fading. The conductor takes his place in the orchestra pit and the music starts. The curtain rises and the ballet begins. What goes on behind the glamour and the lights we see on stage? Ballet is a wonderful and exciting spectacle for the audience, but it is just about the toughest job on earth for the dancers. Dancers are athletes and must train every day of their dancing lives. Although there could not be a ballet without dancers there are many other specialists who together work relentlessly with one goal in mind—the ballet. In this book you can find out just how much hard work is needed to become a dancer; the preparation leading up to the first night; the stars; the ballets and some of the world's famous ballet companies. The lavish illustrations have been selected carefully to blend completely with the text which is easy to read and has been checked by experts of the ballet world. *Discovering Ballet* is perfect for all young readers between the ages of 9-14 who love ballet and want to know what goes on behind the stage curtain.

In association with
The Royal Ballet

Cover: Pupils of The Royal Ballet School, White Lodge.

Overleaf: Boys of The Royal Ballet School, White Lodge.

Left: London Contemporary Dance in *Polonaise.*

ENIGMA

Author: Robin May
Adviser: Mary Clarke
editor of *Dancing Times*
Editor: Trisha Pike
Art Editor: Adrian Gray
Picture Researcher: Julia Calloway

Special thanks go to the teachers and
pupils of The Royal Ballet School,
White Lodge for all their help.

This volume is not to be sold
outside of the United States
of America and Canada.

Published by Marshall Cavendish
Children's Books Limited,
58 Old Compton Street,
London W1V 5PA

© Marshall Cavendish Ltd. 1979
First Printed 1979

Printed in Great Britain

ISBN 0 85685 680 0

All photographs are by Reg Wilson except:
All Sport/John Starr 48(l), 68(t), back cover,
Courtesy of Australian Ballet 46-7,
Courtesy of The Australian Information
    Service, London 71,
BBC Copyright Photograph 12(t), 36(t),
Courtesy of Cunningham Dance Foundation 72(t),
Daily Telegraph Colour Library 42(l), 48-9,
Zoe Dominic 14-5(t), 33(b), 46(l),
Courtesy of Nederlands Dans Theater 74(t), 75(t),
Novosti Press 12(b), 13, 35(b), 62-3,
Courtesy of Opéra de Paris 14-15(b),
Courtesy of Royal Danish Ballet 15,
Leslie E. Spatt 34(t),
Martha Swope 37, 66,
Courtesy of Tokyo Ballet 56-7,
Jack Vartoogian 6, 7, 32, 47(r), 49, 67, 70, 72,
Jennie Walton 39(t),
Angela Williams 26-7,
Astrid Zydower 38(t).

Illustrations
Institute of Choreology 42,
Valerie Littlewood 10-1, 28-9, 40-1, 52-3, 64-5,
Ian Spurling 44-5,
Tony Streek 50-1.

Contents

★ ★

Left: Louis Falco Dance
Company in *Tiger Rag*.

Below: Alvin Ailey
Company in *Butterfly*.

Foreword

★ ★ ★ ★ ★ ★ ★ ★ ★ ★ ★ ★ ★ ★ ★

It has given me great pleasure to co-operate with the people responsible for producing this book as I believe they have succeeded in giving a true picture of life in the world of ballet. *Discovering Ballet*, all the time, recognizes the dedication that is required not only from young students but also from professional dancers throughout their careers. In taking you into the classroom and behind the scenes the book explains all the hard work that has to be done before a ballet performance can take place. Yet it does not destroy the magic of the actual performance in the theatre. Rather, you are led, as young dancers are led by teachers, on that exciting journey from the toil of daily practice to the wonderful moment just before the curtain rises when everything comes together to make the finished ballet. This book gives you understanding and therefore a sense of involvement in the life of a ballet company and a ballet school.

I hope that after reading *Discovering Ballet* young members of the audience will enjoy ballet even more. Because it is for you, the audience, that everyone in ballet schools and ballet companies works. Our duty is to give you pleasure and your enjoyment is our reward.

Barbara Fewster
Director of Balletic Studies, The Royal Ballet School
Fellow of the Imperial Society of Teachers of Dancing

Left: Girls of The Royal Ballet School, White Lodge.

9

TRAINING FOR THE TOP

★ ★

The Hard Life

There is one fact of ballet life that may surprise you.
Although ballet is exciting and romantic for the audience, it
is just about the toughest job on earth for the dancers. Of
course, you don't have to be a heavyweight champion to be a
dancer, or swim the Channel, but you have to train harder
than any athlete in any sport. You also have to be fitter than a
lumberjack or a star footballer. Yet some people still think
that ballet is just a pretty entertainment. Some even think it
an odd profession for a man. However, the Russians and the
Danes think it natural for a man to dance. Of course, they are
right to think so.

Dancers must train every day of their dancing lives, except
on a rest day or the annual holiday. Their all-important daily
class usually starts at 10.30 in the morning and lasts for
about an hour and a half. During this period they must bend
and stretch their bodies into shape for dancing. There is no
shirking for anyone, whether they are stars or students.
Ballet training needs the courage to keep going even when it
hurts and the determination to succeed.

Doctors examine young hopefuls very thoroughly before
they are accepted by a ballet school. This is because any

★ ★

weakness in the body must be spotted at once to prevent later disappointment. Yet for some who cannot meet the demands of ballet they can still enjoy the thrill of dancing in theatre shows or musical comedy.

At vocational or state ballet schools around the world likely children get educational schooling as well as ballet training. This training goes back centuries and ensures that balance, control and the correct distribution of the body's weight are all attained. It also develops the skill of the feet and legs. At about the age of 12, girls go up on *pointe*: they are not usually strong enough earlier. The boys do regular gymnastics as an absolutely vital part of their training. Yes, there is plenty to learn before reaching the age of 16, when full professional training will begin.

The daily class for everyone from beginners to ballerinas is the perfect means for getting the body warmed up. It begins with the first gradual movements at the *barre* and ends with spectacular leaps by the men and wonderful pointe work by the women. Then, if a dancer is with a company, it will be time to rehearse. If a student, it will be back to ordinary schoolwork or further practice with the hope that one day he or she will get into a company.

11

Learning the Russian Way

★ ★

Our first look at training methods around the world must be in Russia. Readers will have plenty of chances to find out why Russia's place in ballet history is unique. This means that the schooling of its dancers down the years must have been very fine. For every great company can only be great if it is firmly founded on excellent schooling at the start of every dancer's career.

Training in Russia dates back to 1738 when the Imperial Theatre School was founded. The ballet master, a Frenchman named Jean Landé, had come to St Petersburg (now Leningrad) in 1734. So expertly did he teach dancing to poor children at their school that the Empress Anne took an interest in him, with historic results.

His first pupils at the Imperial school were children of the Empress's servants. Much later, this school was to become the Kirov Ballet's famous school. Down the years a superb system of dance training was developed, not only in St Petersburg, then the Imperial capital, but also in Moscow, now home of the great Bolshoi Ballet company.

In 1917, the Russian people rebelled against their rulers but the Revolution did not see the end of ballet, as some had feared. Indeed, the Imperial tradition remained strong in what became Leningrad. Today, more than 60 years after the Revolution and the end of the aristocracy, dancers trained in Leningrad at the Kirov school (as it is called for short) are renowned for their aristocratic style as well as their wonderful lightness of movement.

The Bolshoi's magnificent dancers, some of whom are capable of the most spectacular and acrobatic feats of ballet, are also very finely trained. Both the Kirov and the Bolshoi companies inherited the system devised by a teacher of the old Imperial Ballet. She was Agrippina Vaganova, who died in 1951.

One special feature of Russian training is extra work on the back, so that many dancers can arch it backwards during leaps with thrilling results. If Leningrad's dancers seem the most satisfying to the expert ballet-lover, both great companies show that Russia's teachers are as magnificent as ever they were.

As for the pupils, after their years of training, the most exciting event in their student careers is their final Graduation Examination in Dance. In front of famous and powerful figures in the ballet world, they show what they have learned, and what promise they have for the future.

Right: The main picture shows a big moment in the life of young Russian students. The place is Vladivostock to the far east of Russia and the dancers are students of the ballet school there. This is their annual performance and they are performing *Maritime Souvenir.*

Left inset: Boys of the Bolshoi Ballet school hard at work.

Right inset: Two young pupils of Leningrad's great Kirov school.

12

★ ★

European Training

★ ★

In Denmark

Denmark is a country which excels especially in one art. Fortunately for us that art is the ballet! Its excellence, and therefore the excellence of the training methods at the Royal Danish Ballet School in Copenhagen, is due to a great Danish choreographer, August Bournonville (1805-79), many of whose works are still danced. You can read about one of them, *La Sylphide*, on page 54.

About 200 would-be ballet dancers attend the entrance examinations held every year at the Royal Danish Ballet School. After a nine-year course, only a handful can hope to be engaged by the company itself. However, all the pupils will have had a training based not only on the traditions of Bournonville, but also on more modern methods. These date from 1930, when a former dancer, Harald Lander, returned home at a time when the company was at rather a low ebb. He brought with him Russian methods and other ideas, which widened the company's range and its teaching methods. Above all, he engaged the great teacher Vera Volkova who helped the company win international fame.

Later, Flemming Flindt brought in even more modern works, transferring television ballets to the stage and doing pop musicals. When he left in 1978 the Danes began to

Right: In very grand surroundings, the boys of the Paris Opéra school practise under the eagle eye of their teacher.

Below: These boys and girls of the Paris Opéra school are here displaying their abilities as a group. Some will become stars but most will become members of a company's important *corps de ballet*.

Below left: A group of lucky children, for they attend the Royal Danish Ballet School. Although they will train for nine years, only a few of them can hope to be engaged as dancers.

re-establish their Bournonville inheritance. They have proved their versatility in dance styles and they have also a wonderful tradition of mime (silent acting).

Once dancers graduate into the company they can spend their whole working life with it. If too old to dance, they take mime roles or teach.

and France

Ballet has been presented at the Paris Opéra longer than anywhere else for reasons you will find on page 52. Not in the building that stands so majestically today in the heart of Paris but in various other theatres that came before. Louis XIV, the Sun King, loved ballet and danced in court entertainments. In 1669 he gave permission for the building of the first Paris Opéra (in a converted tennis court) and its school was established in 1731. All the great names in ballet history from its beginnings until today have been associated with the Paris Opéra. Marie Taglioni triumphed there (see pages 28 and 54) and Yvette Chauviré, a great star and contemporary of Margot Fonteyn, now teaches there. Serge Lifar, the great Russian dancer and choreographer, restored the importance of French ballet during the 1930s and 1940s. The school is still very famous.

Life with The Royal Ballet School

★ ★

In January 1931 Ninette de Valois (whom you can read about on page 39) founded a ballet company. As a key part of that company a ballet school also opened at Sadler's Wells Theatre in London. Today, nearly 50 years later, it is now called The Royal Ballet School and, like any good ballet school, it is the foundation on which any great company must always be built.

There are about 120 pupils at The Royal Ballet Lower School at White Lodge in Surrey, aged from 11 to 16. The pupils are assessed every year to make sure they come up to standard. At 16 students who are good enough go to the Upper School, along with boys and girls from other dance schools in Britain and overseas. The Upper School is at Baron's Court, London and instructs about 150 pupils.

You may wonder if the fees are high. But there is no need for concern. No British boy or girl is kept away from The Royal Ballet School because there is a shortage of the necessary money at home.

Naturally, ordinary schooling is given to the ballet pupils right through their training. However, Upper School pupils may also continue to study for their general exams, just like other schoolboys and girls. This is particularly valuable to those students who aim to become ballet teachers. At The Royal Ballet School there is a three-year teachers' training course for them.

However, the School's main job is to supply The Royal Ballet and its touring company, Sadler's Wells Royal Ballet, with new talent. Once they have graduated, the students may be lucky enough to join The Royal Ballet or Sadler's Wells Royal Ballet; if not they can go to companies in Britain and elsewhere. If they are among the lucky ones they will be following in the footsteps of most of the principals, soloists and members of the *corps de ballet* of The Royal Ballet at Covent Garden, and Sadler's Wells Royal Ballet, who also started their training at the internationally famous Royal Ballet School.

Above right: These boys are hard at work under their instructor. He trains with a dumb-bell and one day they will, too, but now they use sticks. Famous dancers of the past look down on them from pictures on the walls! During their training the boys work harder and more steadily than almost any sportsman. To be a male dancer you have to be tough as well as graceful.

Right main picture: Girls of The Royal Ballet School working at the barre. All their working day is organized to the exact minute. The discipline of the ballet world begins young and never ends.

Below right: The boys and girls of the Lower School rehearse together for an end-of-year performance. As a rule, however, they do their training apart.

Below left: Another glimpse of the girls hard at work under the careful guidance of a teacher.

The Famous Five

★ ★

The famous five basic positions of the feet have a long
history. They go back more than 300 years. They were
written down by a Frenchman named Beauchamps in the
late 17th century, but it is thought that they were being used
before he did so.

Why are these positions so important ? The answer is
that training cannot begin until they are mastered. For each
position the feet have to be turned out from the hip. By

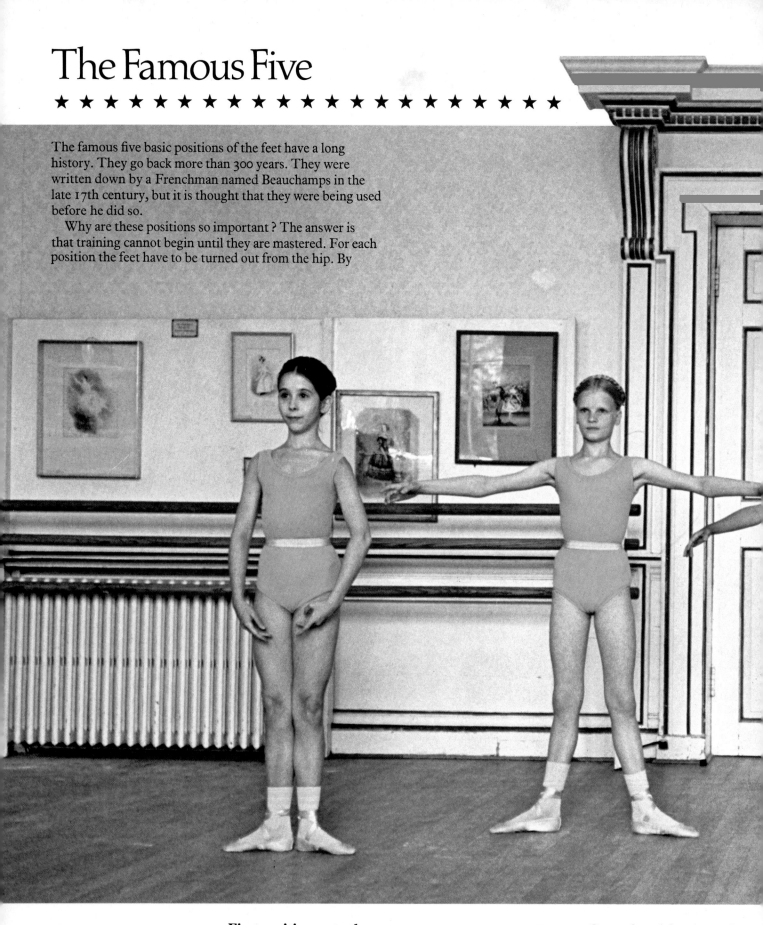

**First position: note that
the legs are together and
heels are touching, but
do not overlap. The feet
are in a straight line.**

**Second position: now the
feet, still fully turned out,
are about 50 centimetres
apart and the weight of the
body is evenly distributed.**

turning the leg outwards from the hip to 180 degrees the dancer has freedom of movement and an elegant appearance. However, this is difficult to accomplish and beginners have to take things slowly.

Pictured here are the five positions with which nearly all the steps in classical ballet begin and end. They were worked out to make sure that a dancer's balance will be perfect with the body in any position.

Third position: look at the way the turned-out feet have the heel of the front foot 'locking' into the back foot's instep.

Fourth position: there are two versions. The one shown here is an extension of the fifth position. The feet are 25 centimetres apart.

Fifth position: notice that the feet are together. The joint of the big toe of the back foot can be seen just beyond the heel of the front foot.

Who Needs Words?

★ ★

Acting without words is a vital part of a dancer's job. This is because feelings have to be conveyed without using speech. Of course, the dancer is trained to express himself or herself with the body throughout the whole of every ballet. However, there are movements in a ballet when a set of gestures are used to put across the story. These gestures are part of the sign language of mime which is understood all over the world. In the same way, Red Indians on the Great Plains of North America all understood each other, however different their language, because they used a sign language which every tribe understood.

During the past centuries the language of ballet has developed its own mime. It reached a climax in the 19th century with works such as *Giselle*, *Coppélia* and *Swan Lake* in which mime was almost as important as the dancing. Early in the 20th century, the great Russian choreographer Mikhail Fokine (you can read about him on page 29) decided to use not mime but gestures that were more natural, lyrical and flowing. Others followed his lead, but you can still see mime used in the popular 19th century classics, so it is useful to know what some of the mime gestures mean.

Whole sentences can be spelt out by using mime, such as 'I Love You'. However, shown on this (the next) page are single statements. You will be able to see that most of them are easy to identify. This is because they are based on real life gestures and understanding them is common sense.

Love: the hands of the dancer are placed over the heart.

Hear: two hands are used to indicate the dancer's ears.

Ask: the hands are clasped together in an imploring gesture.

20

See: one hand is placed on the eye to indicate sight.

Fear: the hands are used to suggest the warding off of evil.

Marry: shown by a finger pointing at the wedding ring finger.

No: the hand makes a pushing gesture, and the head turns away.

21

Working Clothes

★ ★

What do dancers wear during that long daily class described on page 10. The normal practice dress for girls is tights and either leotards or tunics; for boys it is tights and sweat shirts. At the start of a class some of the dancers wear woollen cross-over bodices and thick knitted leggings (known as leg-warmers). These extra clothes help to keep the unexercised muscles warm. They will be discarded as the dancers get warmer and warmer the hard way.

The girls must have their hair neatly bound for classroom work, so that the teacher can see their neck muscles. In fact, there are two important points concerning practice dress. One is that teachers must be able to see the body and so spot mistakes at a glance. The other is that dancers must have complete freedom of movement and not be worried that some article of their clothing might slip or snap.

The most essential clothing items for any dancer are, of course, the shoes. This is especially true of the girls who, like the boys, use leather slippers, but also the satin pointe shoes for dancing on the tip of the toe. In ballet's early days

Below: You can see here how a dancer will bend the stiff leather back of her shoe. It has to be done very gradually until finally it becomes flexible.

Above right: Girls at The Royal Ballet Lower

School take a quick break in class to tie their tapes. Note the neat leotards. The girls are wearing socks but next year will wear tights. The colour of their belts will change as they move higher up the school, reaching towards their goal.

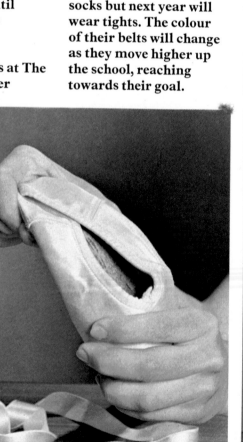

there were no special pointe shoes. Dancers merely padded their shoes with cotton wool and darned the toes of their shoes to stop them slipping and sliding on the floor. From the 1860s onwards, shoes were blocked or stiffened with glue to give them strength and support.

Naturally, a girl's pointe shoes must be chosen and fitted with great care. She might break down the block to make it more pliable. Also she might bend the shoe's stiff leather back for the same reason. She will sew on her own ankle ribbons to ensure that the shoes feel secure when she is dancing. After a great deal of hard use the shoes might need reblocking. This is done by pouring some special liquid glue into the shoe and rolling it round with care so that the old block is coated. About 12 hours later it has hardened and the blocked shoes are ready to take the strain again.

Do men ever dance on pointe ? It is very rare indeed, though it sometimes happens. For example, in *The Dream*, when Bottom is changed into an ass he dances on pointe to give the impression of prancing on hooves.

Below left: A dancer sews on her own tapes. She alone knows where the tapes will feel most comfortable for her feet. Also, by doing the job herself she can be certain that her shoes will stay securely tied throughout a performance.

Below: Breaking down the block of a pointe shoe to make it more pliable has to be done expertly. It is no job for a beginner until she has received some instruction, for otherwise the shoes will be spoiled. Note the knocking process.

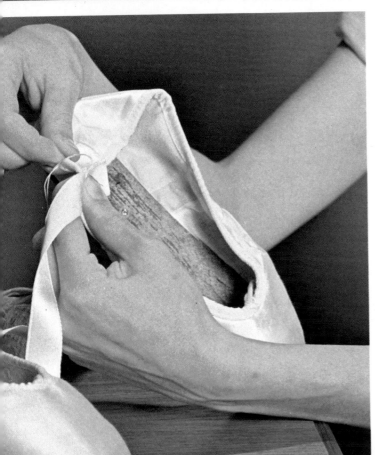

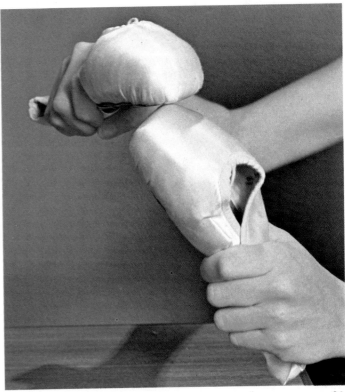

Making the Most of Your Face

★ ★

Make-up is an art all stage folk have to learn. The ordinary stage make-up is the basic one with which the dancer, or actor, or opera singer projects his or her own face to an audience. It is no use going on stage in a big theatre with strong lighting and expecting your normal face to be clearly seen, because it won't. With a basic stage make-up the features of the face are exaggerated so that they can be easily seen by the audience. The eyes especially need very good highlighting. Girls are at an advantage here as they are usually experts at make-up anyway. If you see a made-up dancer at close range the make-up looks overdone as a rule. However, it isn't from an audience's point of view.

Make-up becomes more difficult when a dancer plays a character part. The part might be a witch, wizard or old person. Nose-putty will probably be used to create a hook-nose or one with warts. There will be lots of lines and smudges, all carefully highlighted and shadowed to look like wrinkles. Look at some famous portraits by great artists and you will see how they highlighted and shaded their subjects' faces to get the right effect.

Sometimes a male dancer will play a female part, such as a witch or an Ugly Sister. But whether it's a male or female dancer playing the character part the chances are he or she will have to disguise a handsome or pretty face with an ugly one. This is part of the fascination of make-up.

Below: Derek Rencher of The Royal Ballet is seen here with a foundation make-up on, ready to start turning himself into the evil Kostchei who appears in *The Firebird.*

Top right: Now he has highlighted his eyes and cheeks in an exaggerated way, put on a false chin and putty to make his nose look larger.

Right centre: On goes a splendid beard.

Below right: He pulls on his talon gloves.

Far right: The final result, which will look superb to the whole audience, whether in the front row or gallery.

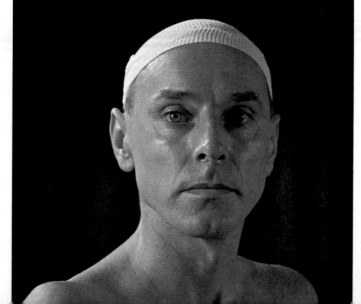

Touring -the Pleasure and the Pain

★ ★

So now you've finished student training, as far as a ballet dancer ever finishes training, and you've got yourself a job. Maybe it is with a touring company. Maybe, the company is off to Europe, stopping to perform at romantic places such as Venice. More probably it will be the sort of tour that takes you to an industrial town in northern England! There a wet Sunday afternoon in November finds you and most of the rest of the company looking for theatrical 'digs' in the rain.

As more and more theatres have closed because of the high cost of running tours and the cost of maintaining the buildings, so, too, alas, have many theatrical digs vanished. These are the lodgings that cater especially for theatre folk. Their owners understand performers' problems and provide that all-important hot meal late at night after the show. Dancers always need a good meal after a performance. They are very hungry by then, it is their main meal of the day and the one they enjoy most!

Sometimes dancers have to sleep in the theatre or on trains, if a new city or town is being visited every night. If it is a small company, the dancers will be performing not in theatres, but in church, village or school halls. These will also be used for rehearsals and may be cold, damp and dingy. Naturally, when you are young and keen this can all be great fun, especially the thrill of bringing ballet to new audiences. But 'one night stands' are tough in the hard world of ballet.

Some dancers go straight into a resident company, but most will have their share of the extra rigours of touring. Although it is a good way of seeing your own country and, for the lucky ones, the world, the daily routine of class, rehearsal and performance goes on. There is a saying among dancers: 'If you miss a class for one day, you know it, if you miss a class for two days the audience will know it.' Star or student, it is all the same.

Below and right: Behind-the-scenes glimpses of Sadler's Wells Royal Ballet on tour.

Above: The beauty and poise of the dancers on stage gives no inkling to the audience of the cramped dressing-rooms that even the stars have to use.

★ ★

Below: Although her new shoes are a little too big this member of the *corps de ballet* knows how to make them fit. With only moments to go before curtain-up she wets the back of her shoes. Water makes the shoes shrink so that they fit closely on her heels.

Below: A quiet moment during a strenuous day.

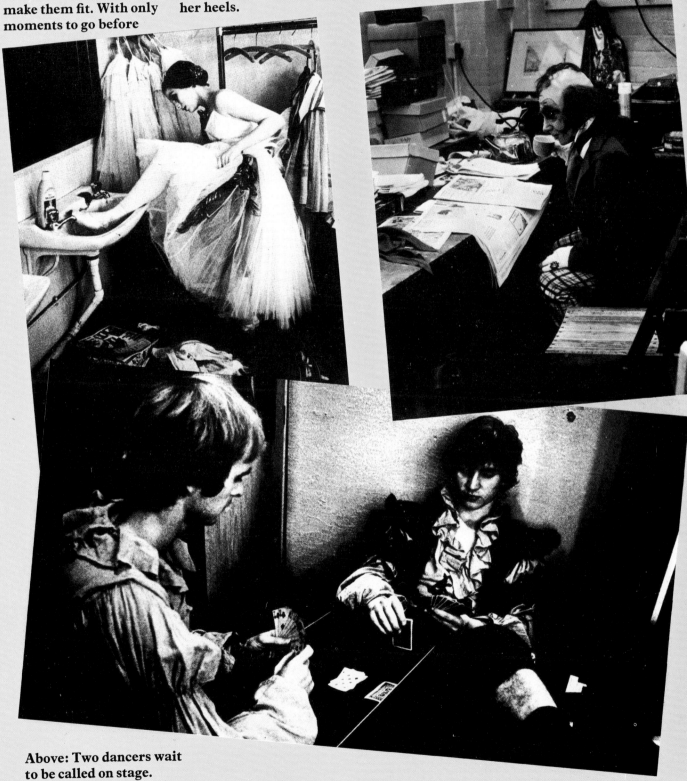

Above: Two dancers wait to be called on stage.

HALL OF FAME

★ ★

Romantic Queen

Marie Taglioni was the queen of ballet in its Romantic age.
She was born in Sweden in 1804 and her father, Filippo, was
an Italian ballet-master. He was a stern teacher and made her
work till sometimes she collapsed with exhaustion. However,
it paid results. Her feet and ankles were so strong she was
among the first to dance on pointe, to the amazement of all.
She made her debut in 1827, then five years later, had such a
success in *La Sylphide* in Paris that she, and the ballet,
changed history. (You can read about it on page 54.) She
danced to packed theatres everywhere. Her audiences loved
her for her lightness, charm and grace: she even seemed to
float in the air. Her hairstyle, parted in the middle, became
traditional for dancers.

The World's Ballerina

Anna Pavlova was one of the greatest and most beloved
dancers in ballet history. Born in Russia in 1881, she was a
star of the Diaghilev Company (which you can read about on
page 64). Then she became world famous touring with her
own company, bringing ballet to thousands who had never
seen it. Her most popular dance was *The Dying Swan*. She
was not just a light, graceful ballerina of genius: she was also
a dancer who, more than anyone else in her time, made
people aware of the beautiful world of ballet. Like Taglioni,
she was poetry in motion, and she left the world a glimpse of
her work in some fragments of film.

Anna Pavlova

Marie Taglioni

★ ★

Vision of a Genius

Mikhail Fokine, born in Russia in 1880, was a choreographer of genius who helped to make the Diaghilev ballets not just famous but revolutionary. Fokine created a new style of ballet, where dancing, scenery, costume, music and acting were all important. He believed that ballet was a serious art and not just a pleasant way of passing the time. His masterpieces included *Les Sylphides*, *Petrushka* (his finest work) and *The Firebird*. He died in 1942 leaving a style of choreography that inspired the ballet world.

Nijinsky—The Legend

Vaslav Nijinsky was a Russian. Born in 1889, he was a superstar before the word was invented, and the most famous male dancer of his day. He merged totally with his roles. Such was his genius that he convinced people that he could pause at the top of his amazing leaps! The clown Petrushka was his most famous role. He not only made his name as a dancer but as a choreographer, especially with his *L'Après-midi d'un faune* (The Afternoon of a faun) in which he danced the lead. However, his revolutionary *Rite of Spring* caused commotion on its first night in Paris in 1913. The audience, stunned by Igor Stravinsky's strange music and Nijinsky's unusual choreography, were in an uproar nearly all the time, some of them even fighting with each other. Yet though little of the music could be heard, many realized that they were witnessing a masterpiece.

Vaslav Nijinsky

Mikhail Fokine

Living Legends

★ ★

Margot Fonteyn

She has been a star for more than 40 years. In fact, Margot Fonteyn has been a star since her early days with the Sadler's Wells Ballet, now The Royal Ballet company.

Born in 1919, Fonteyn has been admired and loved for her artistry, her beauty and theatrical flair, and her exquisite line, ever since she became a ballerina in 1935. At that time she took over many of the roles that Alicia Markova had danced at Sadler's Wells Theatre. Her first famous partnership was with Robert Helpmann (now Sir Robert). This partnership contributed so much towards the boom in British ballet in the late 1930s and 1940s. In 1946 they starred together in *The Sleeping Beauty*, which marked the reopening of the Royal Opera House, Covent Garden after the war, and the company's transfer there.

Soon Margot Fonteyn (Dame Margot from 1956) was conquering the ballet world. Then, just when it seemed that her greatest days were over, she began her most famous partnership of all with the young Russian exile, Rudolf Nureyev. It started in 1961, one of many glorious results being *Marguerite and Armand*, choreographed by Sir Frederick Ashton. Today Fonteyn no longer dances the great roles of her glorious past but her name is a household word, and she is a legend in her own lifetime. For the record, her first major role was in Ashton's *Le Baiser de la Fée* (The Fairy's Kiss). A matchless career was underway.

Above: Margot Fonteyn as the heroine in *Raymonda,* **to music by Glazunov.**

Below: Fonteyn and Nureyev at the Capulets' ball in *Romeo and Juliet.*

Rudolf Nureyev

Rudolf Nureyev was a star in his native Russia with the Kirov Ballet before hitting the headlines in 1961 when he left the company as it toured France. He had been starring in *The Sleeping Beauty* with great success.

He was born in 1938 on a train journey between Lake Baikal and Irkutsk. He had studied at the Kirov school, Leningrad before joining the Kirov Ballet. There he ran into trouble with the authorities. The result? He decided to leave during that fateful French tour and Russia's loss was the West's gain. In particular, The Royal Ballet gained, as he immediately became their permanent guest artist. He danced exclusively with the company for five years. His thrillingly brilliant style, electrifying personality and the sense of excitement he brought on stage made his every appearance an event. As we have seen, it was with Margot Fonteyn that he first captured the hearts of British ballet-lovers. By the mid-1960s, he was a famous choreographer as well. The United States, Canada, Australia, Italy and elsewhere have all hailed him as superb. Even now, when younger rivals challenge his supreme position, his tremendous stamina lets him dance night after night.

Nureyev has also put his talents on film. These include his *Don Quixote* production with the Australian Ballet and frequent appearances on television. He has thrilled millions of people who have never seen a 'live' ballet performance.

Above: Rudolf Nureyev as the Prince in *The Sleeping Beauty*, one of the many **roles he danced with Fonteyn at the Royal Opera House.**

Superstars of Today and Tomorrow

★ ★

Natalia Makarova

Natalia Makarova was born in Russia in 1940. Her wonderful elegance and nobility are, of course, her own, but also show what superb training she had at that greatest of Russian schools, the Kirov in Leningrad. Her figure is perfection and many people consider her the top female dancer in the whole world of ballet today.

She joined the Kirov Ballet in 1959 and she was soon a star. However, she felt she could not progress enough in Russia, which is now short of top choreographers and where officialdom can hamper an artist's progress. So when the Kirov Ballet company was visiting London in 1970, she decided to live in the West. By her decision her country lost a very great dancer.

She first danced with The Royal Ballet in 1972, but most of her dancing has been with American Ballet Theatre. She is supreme in classical roles such as Giselle, but is also breathtaking in more modern works. As for her Juliet in Kenneth MacMillan's *Romeo and Juliet*, many consider it faultless. So was her Manon in his ballet of that name. One of her most famous partnerships was with her fellow Russian, Mikhail Baryshnikov.

Right: Makarova as the Firebird, one of her roles for American Ballet Theatre.

Mikhail Baryshnikov

'Misha' (as he is nicknamed) was born in 1948 in Riga, Russia, and his first training was at the Riga Choreographic School. In 1967 he joined the Kirov Ballet and was soon one of the most exciting dancers in Russia. He originated the title role in Konstantin Sergeyev's *Hamlet*, the first major creation of many.

In 1974, while on tour in Canada he decided he wouldn't go back to his own country. He joined American Ballet Theatre and was a sensation. Although shorter than some male dancers, he has Vaslav Nijinsky's gift for seeming to defy the laws of gravity. Technically, he is astounding, as dazzling a dancer as has ever appeared before the public. He is also a fine actor, as the millions of cinema-goers who have seen the film *The Turning Point* will agree.

His partnership with Makarova was an instant ballet legend, when they danced that classical showpiece, *La Bayadère*. Such is Misha's genius that, having been brilliant in this, he can switch to being wildly funny in a work like Twyla Tharp's *Push Comes to Shove*.

Right: Baryshnikov performs in *Nutcracker*, American Ballet Theatre's production in New York. The ballet was one of many triumphs.

32

Anthony Dowell

He is Britain's first internationally famous male star. His style is everywhere regarded as perfection. A word often used about him is 'noble'. This is because his performances fit perfectly into that ballet category: *danseur noble*.

Born in 1943, he trained at The Royal Ballet School, joining The Royal Ballet company in 1961 and becoming a principal in 1966. A cold way, perhaps, of describing the birth of a star. At a time when few actors can play princes with total conviction, Anthony Dowell is a prince to the manner born: handsome, elegant, aristocratic.

His long partnership with Antoinette Sibley, in *Romeo and Juliet*, *Giselle*, *Manon* and so many other ballets, is now a ballet legend. Frederick Ashton and Kenneth MacMillan have created many roles for him. He was the first Des Grieux in MacMillan's *Manon* opposite Sibley. Later he danced it with equal majesty with Natalia Makarova. Yes, 'majestic' is another word often used to describe Dowell, who was a junior member of The Royal Ballet when Rudolf Nureyev first came to Covent Garden. Years ago critics felt that Anthony Dowell's acting lacked passion. Now his many admirers believe that his art lacks nothing!

Left: Anthony Dowell in Frederick Ashton's *A Month in the Country* at Covent Garden.

Eva Evdokimova

This Swiss-born American dancer was a prima ballerina when she was scarcely in her 20s! Born in 1948 in Geneva, she achieved that high status with the German Opera in Berlin in 1969. British ballet-lovers know her well, too, as a principal with London Festival Ballet. Though she has danced great modern roles, including Juliet in both John Cranko's and Nicolai Boyartchikov's *Romeo and Juliet*, she is best known for her classical performances. Many people find that she conjures up for them the enchanted, now legendary, world of the Romantic era. Her beauty, lyrical qualities and lightness of movement make her Giselle particularly memorable. So, too, are her Aurora in *The Sleeping Beauty* and her Odette-Odile in *Swan Lake*.

Her training was remarkable for it took place in Munich State Opera Ballet School, at The Royal Ballet School, in the Royal Danish Ballet School and in Leningrad, where perhaps her born poise and aristocratic authority were given the extra polish of the Kirov school. There she worked with the great Natalia Dudinskaya, a pupil of Agrippina Vaganova (whom you can read about on page 12). Dudinskaya upholds a tradition that many beleive is the most perfect in all ballet and Evdokimova shows it at its most magical.

Left: Evdokimova in one of her great roles, Odette in *Swan Lake*.

More Superstars

★ ★

Gelsey Kirkland

She is the youngest of the galaxy of stars portrayed on these two pages and the last two. She was born as recently as 1953 and is already regarded by many Americans and others as the most exciting young dancer in the world. Spotted by the great George Balanchine when she was 15, she joined his New York City Ballet in 1968 and became a principal in 1972. Rudolf Nureyev has praised the 'beautiful fluidity in her movements' and been amazed by her extraordinary strength considering 'she is such a small girl'.

Kirkland joined American Ballet Theatre in 1974, and has been partnered by both Nureyev and Mikhail Baryshnikov. It was in Baryshnikov's version of *Don Quixote* in 1978 that she had audiences cheering her spitfire Kitri and that she reached new heights of stardom.

She is a hard worker, even by ballet standards. She lost a part in the film *The Turning Point* because at the time she had become too weak through hard work to sustain roles on stage and looked too gaunt for the screen. She fought back and now she is on top of the world. She is dancing the title roles of Giselle, La Sylphide and many others for which she has audiences moved and thrilled, and cheering.

**Right: The fabulous
Gelsey Kirkland as
Giselle, one of her most
famous roles.**

Galina Samsova

It goes without saying that ballet is an international art, but Galina Samsova's career is even more international than most. Born in Russia in 1937, she trained at Kiev State Ballet School and then joined the Kiev Ballet company as a soloist. Later she married a Canadian dancer and teacher she had met there, Alexander Ursuliak. Together they went to Canada, where she became a ballerina with the National Ballet. From 1964-73 she was London Festival Ballet's ballerina. Then she and her second husband, André Prokovsky, started the New London Ballet, and the pair began to tour. They were a very busy partnership! In fact, they broke away from the idea of a big group to become a small mobile one, performing a wide range of works. Alas, this splendid venture finally foundered. However, Samsova is as busy as ever as a wonderfully lyrical dancer, one of her recent triumphs being her Aurora in *The Sleeping Beauty* in Rome, when her husband was in charge of the Opera's Ballet.

Samsova is the only leading dancer of our time to leave Russia with permission to return, a rare achievement in an age where politics all too often intrude on art!

**Right: Galina Samsova
is raised aloft by her
partner Viktor Róna as
she dances the title role
of *Cinderella*.**

Merle Park

Born in Rhodesia in 1937, Merle Park joined Sadler's Wells in 1954 and became a soloist four years later. After early successes in roles such as Swanilda in *Coppélia*, she played the great roles such as Aurora in *The Sleeping Beauty* and the title role of Giselle. However, her extraordinary technical skill and acting ability gained her roles in many short ballets as well. She created the Celestial in *Shadowplay*, which Antony Tudor choreographed in 1967 on his return after 30 years in the United States. She was also the second ballerina to dance the very demanding role of Lise in Frederick Ashton's *La Fille mal gardée* in 1960. Very different was her Clara in *Nutcracker* for Rudolf Nureyev in 1968, portraying the young girl heroine and brilliantly dancing two taxing *pas de deux* which Nureyev wrote into the work.

Park always brings excitement on to the stage because she dances so brilliantly and swiftly. In 1978, she created the Countess Marie Larisch in Kenneth MacMillan's *Mayerling*, a more mature role than she had previously played, but beautifully portrayed. Her range is as wide as her technique is dazzling and for many years now she has been one of the leading ballerinas of The Royal Ballet. Even in a small role such as the Autumn Fairy in Ashton's *Cinderella*, she can startle and captivate her audience.

Left: Merle Park in *Elite Syncopations.*

Vladimir Vasiliev and Yekaterina Maximova

Both these great stars of the Bolshoi Ballet in Moscow have appeared in the West. Yekaterina Maximova, born in 1939, was coached in many of her roles by Galina Ulanova, her great predecessor. These roles included Giselle in which Ulanova herself excelled.

Maximova is married to Vladimir Vasiliev, who was born in 1940. His heroic and brilliant style and phenomenal energy have amazed and thrilled audiences all over the world. His Spartacus is regarded as the finest yet seen, and in the ballet Maximova often dances the part of his stage wife. Many rank him with Mikhail Baryshnikov as one of the two most exciting male dancers of the late 1970s.

Another ballet in which both Vasiliev and Maximova appear with sensational results is *Don Quixote*, and yet another is *Giselle*. Both have appeared in a number of Soviet ballets never seen in the West. Vasiliev has recently played a very different Petrushka from the usual one for Maurice Béjart's Ballet of the 20th Century in Brussels. He has fine comic ability as well as being the very picture of heroism, while Maximova is a magical dancer with a total devotion to her glorious art.

Left: Vasiliev and his wife Maximova in a thrilling moment in the Bolshoi production of *Spartacus.*

Two Towering Talents

★ ★

Frederick Ashton

Frederick Ashton was born in Ecuador in 1904, far away from the scenes of his later triumphs. When he was a boy he beheld a wonder: Anna Pavlova on tour with her company. He knew at once what he wanted to do in life. Years later, in 1926, he was doing it, choreographing his first ballet, *A Tragedy of Fashion*, in a London show. Britain's greatest choreographer had started on the road to fame. A fame that was to result in works that are already classics, such as *Symphonic Variations*, *Enigma Variations*, *La Fille mal gardée*, *The Dream* and *A Month in The Country*. He was also the choreographer of the film, *Tales of Beatrix Potter*.

Although 'Sir Fred', as he is affectionately known, has worked all over the world, his matchless career has been mainly with the Sadler's Wells/Royal Ballet. He joined it in 1935, working with a rising young star called Margot Fonteyn. From 1963-70 he was The Royal Ballet's director. He inspires dancers and is inspired by their talents. For instance, his enchanting *La Fille mal gardée* was inspired by Nadia Nerina, David Blair, Alexander Grant and Stanley Holden who created the leading roles one magical night in 1960. He holds that rarest of British honours, the Order of Merit. This is as it should be, for his range is as vast as his talent is colossal.

Above: Frederick Ashton talking to Anthony Dowell and Georgina Parkinson.

Below: One of Ashton's many triumphs, a scene from *La Fille mal gardée*.

George Balanchine

Born in Russia in 1904, George Balanchine trained at the Imperial School. However, when he had graduated he found himself in trouble as his ideas were too advanced for his traditionally-minded superiors. On a tour of Germany, he left to join Serge Diaghilev's company, where his genius was soon realized, first in Europe, then, from 1934 onwards, in the United States. For he was invited by Lincoln Kirstein to direct the School of American Ballet, from which the world-famous New York City Ballet later sprang after various triumphs and crises.

That ballet is now booming so remarkably in the United States is due to Balanchine as much as anyone. No one has done more to prove how exciting and moving ballets without a story can be. However, he can also produce stunning versions of old favourites, such as *Nutcracker*, or jolly works like *Stars and Stripes* to Sousa march tunes, in which his dancers became drum majorettes. He used to watch stunt dancers and later included some of what he had seen in his ballets. He is also very musical and was a close friend of Igor Stravinsky. You can read more about his company the New York City Ballet on page 66. In 1964, when they moved to the New York State Theater at Lincoln Center it had naturally been built as Balanchine wanted it.

Above: George Balanchine directing his dancers in *Vienna Waltzes*.

Below: The finished result is a delightful scene from the popular *Vienna Waltzes*.

Creators of Companies

★ ★

Marie Rambert

She was born Myriam Ramberg in Poland more than 90 years ago and she is still a giant in the ballet world to this day. Dame Marie Rambert, as the world knows her, set out to be a doctor, but, fortunately, fell in love with the world of the dance. By 1913, she was helping Vaslav Nijinsky stage *The Rite of Spring* (see page 29).

Her career started in London, where she opened a ballet school in 1920. From this small beginning came the Ballet Rambert. From the start, Marie Rambert showed a genius for spotting talent. These talents included the young Frederick Ashton, Antony Tudor and a host of others down the years. She ranks as one of the founders of British ballet, and one of the most adventurous people in the world of dance. From the beginning she presented modern as well as classical ballets, including Tudor's very popular *Jardin aux Lilas* (Lilac Garden).

Ballet Rambert has become one of Britain's leading modern dance groups. Norman Morrice, now director of The Royal Ballet and the brilliant dancer-choreographer, Christopher Bruce, are two of her modern 'finds'. You don't often see Rambert girls on pointes even though they are classically trained. What you do see is a company living for today and tomorrow, as Marie Rambert does so splendidly.

Below: *for these who die as cattle,* **performed by Ballet Rambert in 1972.**

Right: Although in her 90s Marie Rambert still looks to the future.

Ninette de Valois

When Edris Stannus, as Dame Ninette de Valois was called as a girl, started dancing, there was no such thing as British ballet, let alone a Royal Ballet company. However, the Irish-born girl thought big. It was not enough for her to be a brilliant dancer. Like Marie Rambert, though ten years younger, she wanted to serve ballet by building her own school and company. To do so, she teamed up with another amazing woman, Lilian Baylis, who was already presenting Shakespeare and opera at London's Old Vic Theatre at prices everyone could afford. The Vic-Wells Ballet was to be the result. At first the little company danced both at the Old Vic and Sadler's Wells Theatre but soon was known as the Sadler's Wells Ballet when that theatre became its home.

By the 1940s it was a national glory, and by the 1950s it was an international one. It became The Royal Ballet in 1956. Ninette de Valois (a Dame from 1951) having created one of the world's greatest companies, retired in 1963, though she still takes a very active part in the world of ballet. Tough, dedicated and a born leader, her own ballets include *The Rake's Progress*, *Checkmate* and many others. Frederick Ashton, Margot Fonteyn, Robert Helpmann and a hundred other stars of the world of ballet, along with millions of ballet-lovers, owe her a debt that can never be repaid.

Left: Ninette de Valois, the creator of The Royal Ballet.

Below: A scene from de Valois's *The Rake's Progress*.

BUILDING UP A BALLET

★ ★

A Ballet is Born

The orchestra is tuning up and all over the opera house there is an excited hum of conversation, for it is the first night of a new ballet. Many long weeks of rehearsal have led up to this tense moment. Tense that is for those backstage, for they cannot know how the ballet will be received. The lights fade, the conductor enters the orchestra pit, and soon, moments later, the curtain goes up . . .

How did it all begin ? Sometimes because a choreographer has suddenly had an idea, a vision of what he wants to do, what he longs to put across in movement. More often, he has to come up with a new idea because new productions are so necessary to a ballet company. True, sometimes it may be a new production of a classic, but audience and dancers both need new works. It is the choreographer's job to provide them. Over these and the following pages we will see how he, or she, goes about the mammoth task.

What sort of ballet will it be ? Because the great classics of

★ ★

the past tell stories, many people who are not regular ballet-goers imagine that most ballets have plots. Yet many do not. They may put across a certain mood, for example, happiness, despair and so on. But they may just be about movement. Movements that music has created in the choreographer's mind. One choreographer, an American named Paul Taylor, believes that his ballets are 'food for the eyes', in other words it is the movement that counts.

This is true, of course, however much of a story there is or not. A human body, marvellously used, can make audiences laugh and cry. Add music, add designs and lighting, add a story, an idea, a mood, or just keep up a steady glorious flow of organized movement, and you have a ballet. As long as you also have an audience! For every kind of theatre needs an audience as the final ingredient. The moment comes when the curtain goes up and the ballet begins. But now we must take a closer look backstage at the excitingly difficult task of the choreographer . . .

The Leader

★ ★

A great choreographer is a creative artist in the way that Shakespeare, Beethoven and Rembrandt were creative artists. For the choreographer invents the steps of the ballet and rehearses the dancers, leading them to their goal, the completed ballet. In success or failure he or she is the person in charge even if the dancers sometimes get the biggest cheers of all.

Let us assume that a choreographer has had an idea for a ballet. Perhaps he wants to supply a ballet in which to show off one of his company's dancers, as John Cranko often did at Stuttgart for Marcia Haydée, or as Sir Frederick Ashton so often did for Dame Margot Fonteyn down the years, both at Sadler's Wells Theatre and at Covent Garden.

First the choreographer will look around for the right music. He is rarely able to commission new music because there is usually not enough time. The composer has to have a good deal of time to compose his music. This means the choreographer has to find music that fits his theme, for example Kenneth MacMillan chose Mahler's haunting *Song*

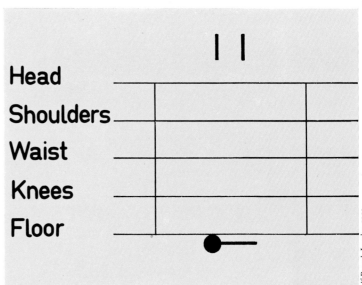

Above: The dancer, the choreographer and the choreologist (seated) work on a new ballet.

Below: This is an example of choreology which is the study of movement through notation.

Above: Before there was movement notation, ballets were remembered and passed on from teacher to student by memory. Today, when a new ballet is created, the choreologist writes down the movements as the choreographer develops his ideas in the rehearsal room. The choreologist uses signs invented by Rudolf Benesh to record the movements. The signs for the hands and feet are placed above, on or below the five lines which represent the top of the head, top of the shoulders, waist, knees and floor. In this way, each position of the body can be noted. This is a notation

of the fifth position as demonstrated by the young student in the photograph on the right. The two vertical signs written above the head line show that her hands are above her head and slightly in front of her body. The horizontal sign shows that her feet are touching, level with her body. The filled-in dot at the left end of the sign shows that her left foot is behind her right. The foot sign is placed below the floor line to show that the dancer is standing with her feet flat on the floor. If the sign was resting on top of the floor line, she would be standing on pointe.

An extract from *Giselle*

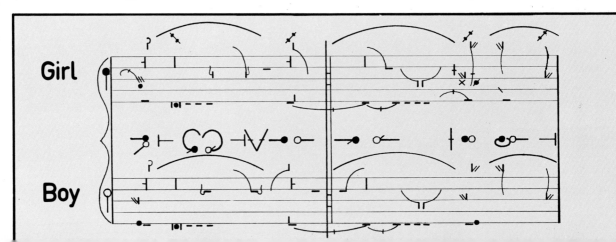

42

of the Earth for his own ballet masterpiece of that name. Of course major works do still get commissioned. Benjamin Britten wrote a marvellous score (musical composition) for John Cranko's *The Prince of the Pagodas*. Usually, however, the choreographer does plenty of listening and thinking before deciding.

Rehearsals have to be fitted into an already busy season. The choreographer may have most things worked out in advance, which has been Dame Ninette de Valois's method during her career but, more probably, he will come to that very first rehearsal with just a few ideas. He will not necessarily start the proceedings at the start of the ballet. He might decide to begin in the middle at an all-important moment which sums up the ballet as a whole. He might even start at the end. It is entirely up to him. Naturally he must be able to demonstrate what he wants, not as perfectly as his dancers will do it. He will be a dancer or an ex-dancer and if he has the right gifts age matters nothing. There are choreographers in their 70s and 80s with much to offer!

Above: Rudolph Nureyev as a choreographer. Here he rehearses some **students from The Royal Ballet School for his** *Nutcracker*.

43

Enter the Designer

★ ★

You can imagine how important the designer is in the making of a new ballet. He will be chosen by the choreographer and will work closely with him throughout rehearsals. Often, he will have worked with the choreographer before, or his work will be well known to him. Sometimes a designer will be chosen by the choreographer from the world of art, as Robert Helpmann chose Leslie Hurry for his *Hamlet* in 1942. Hurry then went on to design many ballets, operas and plays. However, that sort of choice is a risky one, because designing for the stage is a very technical and specialized business.

First the stage settings or scenery have to be worked out and agreed on, after which much of the designer's time will naturally be taken up seeing how the building and the painting of his designs are coming along. He also works with the lighting designer to make sure that the audience sees the scenery at its best.

Next there are the costumes. All theatre costumes pose problems, but ballet has its special problems. Those used in plays and operas, whether historic or modern, are not usually so very different from actual clothes worn by people in real life down the centuries. However, ballet costumes have to be built for dancing. That may sound obvious, but it has to be remembered that ease of movement comes first. Yet the costumes must look right for the part. Also they must be very strong to survive the strains put upon them. Dancers, for reasons that hardly need explaining, sweat constantly and plentifully even in chilly weather. So the costumes have to stand up to that as well.

Finally, comes the first stage call a day or so before the dress rehearsal, and suddenly the whole complicated business of staging a ballet is happening in one spot. Which is a good moment to see how things are going on in the workshops and wardrobe department.

Above: One of many striking costume designs by Leon Bakst. This was created for Nijinsky's role in *Le Dieu bleu*.

★ ★

Below: Some of Ian Spurling's designs for the ballet, *Elite Syncopations,* **which was first seen in 1974, performed by The Royal Ballet.**

Above: Osbert Lancaster the famous cartoonist also works in the worlds of ballet and opera. Here is his Act One *Coppélia* **design.**

Behind the Scenes

★ ★

In the busy, bustling rabbit-warren of a world that is the backstage of a theatre, a new ballet production is only one of the many activities that are happening at any given time. Whatever parts of it may look like, this is a world of order, not chaos. Otherwise not a single ballet or opera would ever be staged. In the paint shop they are busily painting the settings that the carpenters have built to the designer's specifications. Meanwhile, the staff of the costume department are very busy too, hard at work turning the designer's sketches into what the dancers will wear. As we saw on the last pages, the need for movement with ease is vital, and the skilled wardrobe staff know this only too well. They also know that these costumes must always look fresh and clean at every performance.

The Press Office is feeding information to the public about

Left: An artist's designs may originally be drawn very small, but later they have to be painted big and bold for the theatre. Here is scenery for *The Rite of Spring* **being painted by the designer himself, Sidney Nolan, the Australian artist. Designers usually oversee the work and leave the painting to their hard-working staff.**

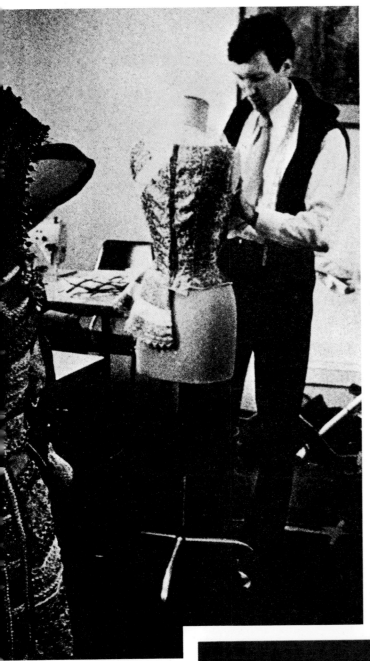

the new production via the newspapers and magazines. There probably will be interviews with the star or stars and with the choreographer in those papers that have arts' reporters as well as critics. Ballet-lovers, especially the balletomanes (those who are ballet enthusiasts), are getting more and more excited as the opening night approaches. Those who cannot buy tickets are becoming desperate!

There are costume fittings before the dress rehearsal, and alterations will have to be made if choreographer or designer or both want them made. Wigs, too, have to be fitted, to make sure they will stay on however spectacular the leaps. In the same way head-dresses are checked to ensure they are secure. The lighting designer is satisfied with his plans which will only be fully revealed when the production has reached the actual stage. Which it almost has . . .

Above: Costumes being made by skilled wardrobe staff.

Right: Makarova having last minute adjustments made to her Firebird costume. Of course, these can only be minor ones with the curtain about to go up on the ballet. There can be no time for anything more elaborate.

Practice Makes Perfect

★ ★

Now the rehearsals of the new ballet are progressing more rapidly. However, they still have to fit in with the daily class and any other rehearsals that are taking place. Sometimes hours of rehearsal will result in just a minute of completed ballet at the end of it. On other days, things go with a swing and whole stretches of ballet will be achieved. Some choreographers will suddenly feel they have been working along the wrong lines and will scrap whole sections of their work and start again. There is no easy way to perfection in any of the arts, theatrical or otherwise.

However, creative genius in ballet and the other arts is a very professional thing. You may have to scrap a section, but there is no time for sitting around and waiting for inspiration. Soon the preparations are all made for the new ballet except the final all-important ones.

Now, the ballet arrives on the stage for the first time. The orchestra is in the pit, the music begins, and probably a tough day will be had by all! There might be trouble with one of the sets, some of the costumes might be wrong, or some of the music might sound very different to the dancers who up to now have only heard it on a piano.

At last, everything is straightened out, and at the dress rehearsal, dancers, orchestra, designs, costumes and lighting are ready to be subjected to a very critical audience. For in the darkened theatre sit the choreographer and his staff and anything still amiss will be noted down and will have to be put right before the first night.

Left: The unending work at the barre, work that has to go on right through rehearsals of a new ballet. It must always be remembered that the dancer's instrument is the perfectly-trained body.

Above: Sometimes a dancer may add a tutu to her practice outfit to give herself the feel of the costume she will later be wearing on stage. Her partner also has to become used to her costume.

Right: Although Baryshnikov and Kirkland are wearing their stage costumes this is still a rehearsal and Gelsey Kirkland wears leg warmers until her leg muscles are warm.

First Night

★ ★

At last the great night has come, and along with it the audience, without whom no ballet can be complete. The theatre begins to fill and the excited hum of talk grows louder and louder as the moment for the curtains to part approaches. The point of no return has been reached. For now nothing more can be done, nothing except a few tiny adjustments to a costume, or a few words of encouragement.

The backstage staff are poised to go into action to ensure the smooth running of the performance. The whole complicated business of lighting the ballet has been tightly organized, right down to those whose job it is to spotlight the stars. Everywhere there is a feeling of tension.

Everywhere that is, except in the audience, for there the atmosphere is electric with excitement. The tension behind the scenes must not be confused with panic. Tension is always present on a first night and it generates another sort of electricity which can produce a great performance.

Among the audience are the ballet critics. What they tell their readers, what the rest of the audience tells its friends, and what later audiences feel, will decide the ballet's fate. The audience may be right or wrong, but the audience, along with the dancers and the choreographer are the real heart of a night at the ballet.

Now, the houselights are fading. The conductor takes his place in the orchestra pit and the music begins. The curtain rises and our ballet begins . . .

Right: The final moments before the curtain goes up on a performance of *Romeo and Juliet*:
1 **Artistic director**
2 **Conductor**
3 **Ballet master**
4 **Dancers**
5 **Technical director**
6 **Stage manager**
7 **Deputy stage manager**
8 **Assistant stage manager**
9 **Lighting manager**
10 **Stage hands**
11 **Props staff**
12 **Security officer**
13 **Fireman**
14 **First aid officer**
15 **Wardrobe staff**
16 **Wigs staff**
17 **Electrician**
18 **Props table**
19 **Scenery dock**
20 **Closed circuit television (to enable the dancers to see the conductor before the curtain rises)**
21 **Cyclorama roll (a backcloth which can be unrolled to surround the back of stage)**
22 **Rosin box**

GREAT BALLETS

★ ★

The Beginnings of Ballet

Ballet was born some 400 years ago in the very grand
surroundings of the courts of Italy and France. The Italians
gave dance entertainments to celebrate battles and marriages.
These were combinations of dance, song and splendid
spectacle and were soon being given in many European
courts. Courtiers would take part in them, looking splendid
in their best clothes, as they formed fine patterns on the
floor of a spacious room or hall.

It was at the court of Louis XIV, king of France in the
mid-17th century that these entertainments became the first
real ballets. The king himself was a fine dancer, although he
got too fat in his 30s to show himself off in public. However,
he saw to it that there was real dance training for the paid
dancers, or professionals, who would soon be taking over

★ ★

from the noble amateurs.

It was now that the five basic positions of the feet were worked out. In fact, so many ballet words were coming into being in France that it is hardly surprising that French is the language used in ballet to describe the steps and movements.

Ballet flowered still further in the 18th century, although at that time, the female dancers wore long dresses and only the male dancers were the big stars. Meanwhile, a great reformer, Jean Noverre, 'the grandfather of ballet' replaced the collection of dances which then made up a ballet with a combination of dramatic dancing and story to make a ballet of action. However, he was less honoured in his own country than elsewhere. Now the 19th century dawned. In about 1820 dancers began to dance on pointe and soon the Romantic ballet would be created.

La Sylphide

★ ★

The Background

The director of the Paris Opéra could not get to sleep. It was the night before the new ballet when several of his dancers would be 'flying' high above the stage, suspended by wires. He was scared something might go wrong. He had taken every precaution and was paying his fliers ten francs danger money. There had been plenty of volunteers, but suppose one fell? He need not have worried, for on the opening night in 1832 *La Sylphide* (The Sylph) had a colossal triumph and its star, Marie Taglioni, (featured on page 28) shot overnight from fame to immortality.

The idea of the ballet had been put to the director, Dr Véron, by the singer Adolphe Nourit, who had read a story of folk being affected by goblins. Véron liked it: it made a change from classical Greek and Roman stories then all the rage. The new choreographer was Taglioni's father, Filippo, and on that wonderful first night Romantic ballet was born. What was Romanticism? It was a movement which swept Europe in the years after the French Revolution. Its sources of inspiration included the supernatural and affected all the arts. Ballet stories that followed *La Sylphide* ceased to be grand and noble and became Romantic.

The Story

In a Scottish farmhouse James dreams of a sylph, a spirit of the air, who hovers over him and kisses him, then vanishes. It is his wedding-day and his fiancée, Effie, arrives. She also is loved by James's friend, Gurn. A witch named Madge proclaims that James does not love Effie, and he drives her away. But when he is alone, his sylph returns and soon they are dancing happily together. They are seen by Gurn, who races to tell Effie. But the sylph has vanished! Later, at a dance, the sylph returns and steals the wedding ring and James runs after her. In the forest where the sylph and her sisters live, Madge gives James a scarf which instead of helping him gain his sylph, kills her. Poor heartbroken James sees Effie going to the altar with Gurn.

The Royal Danish Ballet

This great company, which dates back to 1748, has done more than any other to keep *La Sylphide* alive and popular, for when August Bournonville took charge of the company he gave the ballet a new and matchless production, still used today in Copenhagen and also danced throughout the world. Under choreographers such as Harald Lander and Fleming Flindt the Royal Danish Ballet has become famous also for its modern works (you can read about them on page 14). In keeping with its new policy of modern as well as classical works, famous foreign choreographers have worked with the company, including Frederick Ashton and Glen Tetley.

Below: The evil witch Madge is predicting trouble for James.

Right: Tricked by the witch, James has lost his beloved sylph.

Swan Lake

★ ★

The Background

The management of Moscow's Bolshoi Theatre seemed determined to ruin the new ballet. The choreographer Wenzel Reisinger was incompetent; the conductor Riabov claimed that the music was too difficult; the poor costumes and scenery had been used for other ballets; the ballerina was second-rate and a third of Tchaikovsky's score was removed to make way for inferior music. No wonder *Swan Lake* failed in 1877 and in some later revivals.

It was not until 18 years later that the choreographer Marius Petipa and a fine team did it justice at St Petersburg (now Leningrad) and it triumphed. That was in 1895, but, sadly, Tchaikovsky had died two years before. Ever since, *Swan Lake* has been one of the corner stones of classical ballet. It is a work in which many great ballerinas have thrilled and moved audiences in the great double role of Odette-Odile. It is probably the most popular ballet of all.

The Story

At his coming-of-age party, Prince Siegfried is reminded by his mother that he must soon choose a suitable bride. As he wants to marry for love, he is not pleased. Swans fly overhead and the prince agrees to go hunting with friends. Beside a lake at midnight a group of swans have turned into lovely girls. Their leader, Odette, tells Siegfried how she and her friends have been turned into swans by the evil Rotbart and only at midnight can they become human again for a short while. Siegfried starts falling in love with her but is warned he must be completely faithful and love no other girl. Rotbart plans to stop the lovers. He makes his daughter Odile look like Odette and brings her to a ball. There, Siegfried says he will marry her, while Odette's spirit tries to warn the prince. The final scene by the lake has more than one version. Siegfried is forgiven by Odette but she says they must drown; their sacrifice breaks Rotbart's spell. One version of the ballet has a happy ending; Siegfried kills Rotbart and the lovers are reunited.

The Tokyo Ballet Company

For over a century the Japanese have been eager to learn from the West, and since the ending of the Second World War in 1945, there has been a tremendous surge of interest in Western classical music, ballet and opera. Many Western stars have danced in Japan, but the Japanese saw from the start that they must build up their own ballet companies.

Best of these is the Tokyo Ballet Company, whose head, Tadatsugu Sasaki, asked Olga Tarasova of the Bolshoi Ballet company to train his dancers to perform Bolshoi versions of a number of ballets.

Later, the company's leading dancer, Hideteru Kitahara, took over as artistic director and the company continues to thrive. It has been seen in Europe and in America. The first great star to dance with the company was Maya Plisetskaya of the Bolshoi in 1968.

★ ★

Left: Keiko Kurihashi.

Right: Masako Tohdoh and Chikahisa Natsuyama.

Below: Act Two of *Swan Lake,* **with a great Russian guest star, Maya Plisetskaya.**

The Sleeping Beauty

★ ★

The Background

'Very nice!' said the tsar of Russia condescendingly to the great Tchaikovsky at the end of the first performance of his new ballet, *The Sleeping Beauty*, in 1890. Others, who had much enjoyed the actual ballet, also objected to the music. They preferred the sort of near-trash they often listened to at the ballet. At least the worth of the ballet was recognized, with its wonderful choreography by Marius Petipa, then in his 70s. It was the old man's masterpiece and the role of Princess Aurora is the supreme test of a ballerina in all the classical repertoire.

However, this original version was very costly to mount, as Serge Diaghilev found in 1921 when he lost a lot of money on a magnificent revival in London. He had to cut down to a version which was basically the last act. Happily, the complete ballet was revived by the Sadler's Wells Ballet in 1939 with choreography based on Petipa. The masterpiece had returned to the international repertoire and it was this version, in more a splendid form, that marked the re-opening of the Royal Opera House, Covent Garden in 1946. It contains an endless treasure trove of wonderful dances, set to music that is not merely 'very nice' but incomparable.

The Story

Petipa based his ballet on Perrault's famous story. At her christening Princess Aurora is cursed by the uninvited Wicked Fairy Carabosse, who predicts that the princess will later prick her finger and die. The Lilac Fairy promises that instead she will sleep until wakened by a king's son. When the princess is 16 years old, the disaster occurs after she has danced the great Rose Adagio with her four suitors. A hundred years later finds Prince Charming being told about Aurora by the Lilac Fairy and being sent on his way to her. He finds her and awakens her with a kiss. Aurora's wedding takes place and is celebrated with many dazzling dances.

The Royal Ballet

The Sleeping Beauty has a special place in The Royal Ballet's repertoire. This ballet was the very first to be performed by the company (then called the Sadler's Wells Ballet) in the Royal Opera House, its present home.

Just after the famous 1939 Sadler's Wells production of *The Sleeping Beauty*, war broke out. On tour in Holland in 1940 the company was almost captured by the German invaders. Back home in England their own theatre, Sadler's Wells, had become a rest centre. So the dancers performed at other London theatres and also toured all over Britain. When peace came the company was invited to re-open the Royal Opera House, Covent Garden, which had been a dance-hall during the war. A new production of *The Sleeping Beauty* with Margot Fonteyn and Robert Helpmann, and re-designed by Oliver Messel, was the first of countless triumphs. It was also this production that opened the company's first season at the Metropolitan Opera House, New York in 1949.

Left: The Lilac Fairy, with the wicked fairy Carabosse standing in the background.

Right: The famous Rose Adagio in which Princess Aurora dances with her suitors. Each of them gives her two roses, which explains the name of the lovely sequence.

Below: A hundred years have passed and Prince Charming has been shown a vision of Aurora by the Lilac Fairy and has gone to find her. He awakens her with a kiss and claims her as his bride.

Romeo and Juliet

★ ★

The Background

'What's the matter? Why don't you dance?'
Romeo and Juliet, based on Shakespeare's play, was being rehearsed at Leningrad's Kirov Theatre, and the choreographer Mikhail Lavrovsky had the composer Serge Prokofiev with him. With Konstantin Sergeyev as Romeo and the legendary Galina Ulanova as Juliet the result should surely have been greater than the ballet's first production in Czechoslovakia in 1938 with different choreography. But why did Ulanova sit on a couch and her partner kneel instead of dancing?

The problem was that they couldn't hear the music. This angered the composer and he shouted: 'You want drums, do you, not music?', but Lavrovsky explained that it was so quiet that the dancers could not hear it, and dance. Prokofiev calmed down slightly when he found that by a trick of sound the dancers really couldn't hear the music and said he would rewrite that section. It was a strange landmark in an otherwise uninterrupted road to success. For the premiere in 1940 was a triumph. The ballet is always a great favourite, whether it is Lavrovsky's version, Kenneth

Left: The Masked Ball at the Capulets' house where Romeo and Juliet meet and fall in love at first sight.

Below left: The young lovers are secretly married by the kindly Friar Laurence, as Juliet's nurse looks on.

Below: Revelry in the market place in Verona, a light-hearted moment in the tragic tale.

Below right: There are many rapturous and lyrical scenes for the lovers in this popular and enthralling ballet.

MacMillan's for The Royal Ballet, or others, including John Cranko's for the Stuttgart Ballet, pictured here.

The Story

Most people know Shakespeare's tale of the deadly feud in the city of Verona between the Capulets and Montagues. Romeo, the young son of Montague, goes to a Capulet ball in disguise and meets the even younger Juliet. They fall in love, but against a grim background of hatred and strife, their love ends in tragedy and death.

The Stuttgart Ballet

Germany has never been one of the great dance nations, although ballet has become very popular in the last 30 years. However, at Stuttgart, famous for its ballet in the past, a tremendous upsurge of enthusiasm and talent occurred when John Cranko from The Royal Ballet took over the company from 1960 until his death in 1973. His genius, with dancers such as Marcia Haydée (now the company's artistic director), Richard Cragun and Egon Madsen, took Stuttgart to the top, in *Romeo*, *The Taming of the Shrew* and other ballets.

Spartacus

★ ★

The Background

Not everybody agrees that *Spartacus* is a great ballet, indeed some people are rather rude about it. Like many modern Russian works it has a strong message and an uplifting ending. It is based on the story of Spartacus, the heroic gladiator who led a slaves' revolt against the Romans. A wonderful subject for a ballet, but some complain that it is too much like a film in which the hero is too good to be true and the villain is impossibly bad. However, in the theatre it works and that is what counts.

The first version was given by the Kirov Ballet in Leningrad in 1956, with choreography by Leonid Jacobsen, who cut out all the *pirouettes*, pointe work and so on because of the subject. The fourth and most famous version, pictured here, is by Yuri Grigorovitch and the Bolshoi Ballet company. It is so magnificently danced by the company, with every dancer totally immersed in his or her role, that every audience is swept away by the excitement of it all. Put across like this it is one of the most electrifying experiences of a lifetime. Khatchaturian's music, which is not everyone's idea of a great score, seems right and proper with such dynamic actions happening on stage.

This ballet first burst on the public in 1968 in Moscow, with Vladimir Vasiliev as Spartacus, Yekaterina Maximova as his wife and Maris Liepa as the Roman commander, Crassus, a most villainous scoundrel. Grigorovitch's choreography makes the most of heroes and villains alike and the result is always a triumph.

The Story

Spartacus and his wife are brought to Rome by Crassus, then parted into slavery. He is made a gladiator, but leads a revolt which thousands of slaves join. Reunited with his wife, he is finally defeated and killed, transfixed by spears, dying in his fight for humanity!

The Bolshoi Ballet

Founded in 1776, its roster of great dancers has been colossal. They are renowned today for their vivid, intense performances and the men are hailed for their athleticism. Yuri Grigorovitch is the company's artistic director and chief choreographer. The Bolshoi appeared for the first time in the West in London in 1956, causing a sensation and some of the longest queues ever seen outside the Royal Opera House.

Below: The villainous Crassus holding aloft Aegina, his mistress.

Right: The death of the hero Spartacus, the tragic end of the ballet.

BALLET TODAY

★ ★

The Diaghilev Revolution

Ballet was dead, or so it must have seemed to lively young
dance enthusiasts in Russia and elsewhere around 1900. The
golden days of the Romantic era had given way to a shoddy
decline in standards all over Europe, except in Russia. Male
dancers were out of fashion. In fact, some of their roles were
danced by women! Even in Russia, where there were a few
great ballets and great dancers, the Imperial Ballet was set in
its ways and so were its stuffy audiences. There had to be an
artistic revolution and Russia was the place.

   The man who master-minded it was Serge Diaghilev
(1872-1929). He was not a dancer, but an organizer of genius
and taste. With the artists Alexandre Benois and Leon
Bakst, he and other advanced thinkers planned for the future.
The result was to be The Ballet Russe.

   He first succeeded in Paris with Russian music and opera.
But how could he show off the superbly expressive new
dancers such as Tamara Karsavina, Vaslav Nijinsky and
Anna Pavlova in old productions? Luckily for ballet,

Mikhail Fokine (whom you can read about on page 29) was at hand, ready to stage ballets that were a blend of dance, drama, great music and great painting. The opening night of Diaghilev's season in Paris in 1909 was one of the most sensational in ballet history, especially when the Polovtsian Dances from *Prince Igor* excited the audience to such an extent that they tore off the rail in front of the orchestra.

The best of the new ballets was, perhaps, *Petrushka*, (pictured here) which was first shown in 1912. It starred Karsavina, Nijinsky and Adolph Bolm, with choreography by Fokine, music by Stravinsky and settings by Benois. It is about three puppets at a winter fair in St Petersburg. The clown Petrushka is a tragic, moving figure.

The Ballet Russe, Diaghilev's company, did not go back to Russia after the outbreak of war in 1914 but became the leading company in western Europe, though Fokine and others went their own way. There has never been such a company, such a collection of talent, whose achievements are still felt to this day.

New World of Ballet

★ ★

The New York City Ballet

Founded by Lincoln Kirstein in the mid-1930s, the New York City Ballet did not get its present name until 1948. This renowned company is especially famous for two things: its wonderful ensemble and its even more wonderful choreography by the great George Balanchine. You can read more about him on page 37. Kirstein gave him absolute freedom to do what he wanted and his ballets have ranged from the stark *Agon* (with equally stark music by Stravinsky), to spectacular ballets with a story, such as *A Midsummer Night's Dream*, based on Shakespeare's play.

Another great choreographer, Jerome Robbins, worked with the New York City Ballet, one of his masterpieces being *Afternoon of a Faun* with its haunting Debussy music. But unlike Vaslav Nijinsky, who set the ballet in legendary Greece, Robbins set it in a New York dance studio. His *The Concert* is a very funny ballet in which ten dancers play an audience at a Chopin piano recital and act out their thoughts as inspired by the music. In 1964, the company moved to a new home, the New York State Theater, in the Lincoln Center. One unique event was a week in 1972 devoted entirely to works of Balanchine's friend, Stravinsky.

Below: A colourful scene from *Union Jack*. The ballet is based on British military and theatrical themes. In 1976 George Balanchine produced this work for the 200th birthday of the United States.

American Ballet Theatre

This company started in 1939 when two far-sighted Americans, Richard Pleasant and Lucia Chase, founded a big troupe full of international stars. As their early seasons included the master choreographer Mikhail Fokine and two British talents, Antony Tudor and Andrée Howard, this big thinking paid off. By the middle 1940s the company was very popular and very successful artistically. At that time an American dancer and choreographer erupted on to the scene. He was Jerome Robbins (mentioned above) who was later to create the fabulous musical, *West Side Story*. In 1944, he choreographed his first ballet for American Ballet Theatre. It was called *Fancy Free* and was about three sailors on leave who chase two girls. It was a huge hit and, more important, was an American ballet, as every member of the audience could see. Agnes de Mille's cowboy ballet, *Rodeo*, was another all-American hit as was *Billy the Kid* by Eugene Loring. Both used thrilling music by Aaron Copland. American Ballet Theatre has always been a starry company. We have already met two of them: Natalia Makarova and Mikhail Baryshnikov, formerly of the Kirov Ballet. In 1978 they even signed up Anthony Dowell!

Below: Twyla Tharp's funny ballet, *Push Comes to Shove*. It was first performed by American Ballet Theatre in 1976. Twyla Tharp is a leading American choreographer who works with her own and other companies.

British Ballet-go-round

★ ★

London Festival Ballet

The most famous ballet company started in Britain since the Second World War is London Festival Ballet, once called Festival Ballet. Back in 1949 two superb dancers, Alicia Markova and Anton Dolin, returned home from America and assembled the company which opened in 1950. Its repertoire has been based on popular classics and works from early in the 20th century. These are danced by international guest stars as well as a strong company. It is very popular and its audiences are drawn from a public with wide-ranging tastes in ballet. Today, the company is run by Beryl Grey, once a star of Sadler's Wells Ballet. A very up-to-date item in the repertoire is the two-act *Prodigal Son in Ragtime*, choreographed by Barry Moreland and danced to Scott Joplin music. It is about a young man travelling through the 20th century. This ragtime ballet was an instant hit.

Around the Regions

Western Theatre Ballet, founded in Bristol in 1957 by Elizabeth West and Peter Darrell, aimed to be more contemporary, or up-to-date, by staging ballets, not about fairies and princes, but about human beings with modern problems. In 1962 Elizabeth West died in a mountain accident so Peter Darrell became the sole director. In 1969, the company moved to Glasgow to become Scottish Ballet, presenting modern works and classics cleverly reduced in scale for a small company.

There are many smaller groups now in Britain. The London Contemporary Dance Theatre and Ballet Rambert are discussed on page 73, while Ballet For All, which was founded in 1964, as an offshoot of The Royal Ballet, has toured extensively. Its aim is to bring ballet 'to those who have not seen it, or who may have lacked the chance to do so; and to those who have seen it, but wish to learn more about it.' Northern England is served by Northern Ballet Theatre and soon, with luck, every corner of Britain will at least be able to see ballet occasionally. It is a fine record considering that less than 60 years ago British ballet did not exist.

Above: A striking view of Beryl Grey, artistic director of London Festival Ballet since 1968. When she was with Sadler's Wells Ballet, her starring roles included Odette-Odile, Giselle and Princess Aurora, and before taking up her present post, she danced in many parts of the world including China and Russia. She has given much to the art of ballet.

Below: London Festival Ballet in *Graduation Ball*, a delightful work danced to the music of Johann Strauss. Many other companies have staged this popular piece.

Right: A colourful scene from Scottish Ballet's production of *Herodias*, with choreography by Peter Darrell who has created many ballets for the company.

Commonwealth Dancing

★ ★

In Canada

There was no ballet in Canada before the 20th century, but over the last 40 years there has been an exciting build-up of talent, with the all-important audiences to go with it. The leading company, the National Ballet of Canada, came into being because of the excitement created when The Royal Ballet toured the United States. Britain's Canadian cousins thought why shouldn't they have an international company too? The British dancer, Celia Franca, founded one in 1951 and, after years of hard work, it reached truly high standards. It is helped by a very fine ballet school in Toronto.

The two other big companies in Canada are the Royal Winnipeg Ballet, which dates back to 1939 and Les Grands Ballets Canadiens of Montreal. There is also a modern dance troupe, the Toronto Dance Theatre, which was founded in 1968, and which appeared in London four years later. Ballet is certainly becoming more and more popular throughout this vast Commonwealth country.

Below: The National Ballet of Canada's production of the ever popular *La Fille mal gardée*. Pictured here are Karen Kain and Frank Augustyn, two popular stars of the company.

Below right: Australian Ballet's production of *Petrushka*, a work in the repertoire of many companies. The original choreographer was the great Fokine.

and in Australia

Australia has a far longer history of ballet than Canada dating back to early in the 19th century. Many great performers toured there, including Anna Pavlova. In 1942 a partner of Pavlova, the Czech Edouard Borovansky, formed a company in Melbourne. From the Borovansky Ballet the famous Australian Ballet was founded in 1962, and was also based in Melbourne. Peggy van Praagh from The Royal Ballet was the first director of the young and talented company. Sir Robert Helpmann and Anne Woolliams were later directors. This very attractive company also has its own fine ballet school.

Australian Ballet is based firmly on the classics, but its dancers are very much at home with such wide-ranging talents as the very modern choreographer, Glen Tetley, and his fellow American, John Butler, as well as the greatest choreographers of this century: Frederick Ashton and George Balanchine. Rudolf Nureyev's *Don Quixote*, which has been filmed, is one of their most popular works. The company has toured many parts of the world, including Britain, France, the Lebanon, Canada and South America, and its high standards have been widely admired.

Although Australian Ballet is the country's leading company there are other companies in most of the states. Modern dance is not forgotten and is staged by the Australian Dance Theatre in Adelaide.

Spotlight on Dance

★ ★

The Martha Graham Dance Company

Martha Graham, born in 1894 in Allegheny in the United States, is yet another of the amazing women who have shaped the destiny of ballet and the dance. Before her, the American Isadora Duncan, who had practically no training, paved the way for modern dance by her anti-ballet methods. Martha Graham went further and her many 'dance plays' have made her and her dancers world famous. Once there was a gulf between classical and modern dance, but now each affects the other, even though a classical dancer can change to modern dance but a dancer trained solely in modern cannot switch to the classics. The basic difference between the two is that modern dancers accept the well known law of gravity, while classical dancers aspire to flight.

Merce Cunningham and Dance Company

Born in Washington, Merce Cunningham is an ex-dancer of the Martha Graham Dance Company. In 1952 he founded his own group and developed his own teaching method. His ballets are very modern indeed. One of them, *Un jour ou deux* (One day or two), with equally modern music by John Cage, was actually given an entire evening at the once very traditional Paris Opéra.

Above: The American Merce Cunningham in his own dance *Solo*.

Below: The Martha Graham Company in *The Owl and the Pussy Cat.*

72

London Contemporary Dance Theatre
This exciting company was founded in 1967 with dancers from the London School of Contemporary Dance. The artistic director is the American, Robert Cohan, also an ex-Martha Graham dancer. Although the London Contemporary Dance Theatre has a close connection with the Graham company, the British company has gradually acquired a style and personality of its own and has been acclaimed in the United States.

Ballet Rambert
Marie Rambert, featured on page 38, has always looked forward and not back. Therefore, it is hardly surprising that her company, the oldest British ballet company, went very modern in the mid-1960s when it could no longer afford to stage classical works. The new company was a brilliant group of soloists who have performed many contemporary works, including the ballets of Christopher Bruce. He took the title role in the company's famous *Pierrot Lunaire*, choreographed by the American, Glen Tetley, to Schoenberg's music. With his great talent, and with its dedicated dancers, the company's future looks as bright as its splendid and adventurous past has always been.

Above: The ballet *Polonaise* performed by London Contemporary Dance.

Below: *Pierrot Lunaire*, performed by Ballet Rambert.

European Experiments

★ ★

Maurice Béjart

Sledgehammer theatrical impact is what Maurice Béjart and
his Ballet of the 20th Century bring to performances.
Audiences, including vast numbers of young people, flock to
watch them. This French dancer and choreographer offers
them what they want to see, not only in Brussels, where he
and his dancers have their headquarters, but wherever they
go outside Belgium.

Béjart never worries about the critics. He puts Beethoven's
Ninth Symphony to his own uses, stages colossal spectacles,
such as *Nijinsky, Clown of God*, and ranges from rock music
to Hindu mysticism. His dedicated company dance these
performances in huge tents, sports arenas and halls. Those
people, especially the young, who feel that opera houses are
not for them, can feel at home watching Béjart's ballets. If as
a choreographer he is not as inventive as some, his big, bold,
simple messages certainly get across to everyone.

Nederlands Dans Theater

Holland's modern dance company may not go in for spectacle
along Béjart's lines, but its choreography appeals more to the
average dedicated ballet-lover. A group of young dancers
and choreographers broke away from the Dutch National
Ballet and formed the Nederlands Dans Theater in 1959.
Soon, they were the talk of the ballet world, with
choreographers such as Jaap Flier, Hans van Manen and the
American Glen Tetley, combining classical and modern
ideas. It was not long before they were influencing the rather
traditional National Ballet for the better, and they also
influenced the Ballet Rambert. One ballet in particular made
headlines. This was Tetley's *Mutations* because there were
some nude scenes in it. The company's output was soon
much bigger than most. There were ten new ballet
productions a year. However they were received, all of them
have one thing in common: vitality. That is the company's
hallmark.

With the inspiring story of these two European
experimental companies our book comes to an end. Ballet
lives, not just on past glories but in the present and future.
This is because new roles are always being planned to
challenge dancers and delight you, the audience.

Above right: *November
Steps,* **performed by the
Nederlands Dans Theater.
The choreographer was
Jiri Kylian.**

Right: *Nijinsky, Clown of
God* **by Maurice Béjart was
inspired by the great
dancer, Nijinsky, and
includes glimpses of some
of his most important
and legendary roles.**

Above far right: *Symphony
in D,* **another ballet by Jiri
Kylian and danced by the
Nederlands Dans Theater.**

**Far right: Another scene
from** *Nijinsky, Clown of
God,* **performed by the
Ballet of the 20th
Century. Béjart's
company is based in
Brussels, Belgium and
also tours abroad.**

74

★ ★

Glossary

★ ★

Adagio: This is a dance or a series of exercises in a slow tempo.

Arabesque: A pose in which one leg is extended behind the body with the knee straight and the foot pointed, while the other leg is bent or straight. There are several variations of the arabesque.

Attitude: This lovely position is based on a statue of Mercury by Giovanni da Bologna. The dancer's body is supported by one leg, the other being raised in front or behind and with the knee bent and turned outwards. The arm on the same side as the raised leg is held above the head, the other being extended sideways.

Ballerina: The title given to a female dancer who performs a company's leading classical roles. Sometimes, people outside the ballet world use the term to describe any ballet dancer. This is quite incorrect as it takes many years of hard work and an exceptional amount of talent to reach the position of ballerina.

Balletomane: A fervent ballet-lover who suffers from ballet mania!

Ballon: The springiness of a dancer's feet.

Barre: The wooden bar attached to a classroom wall which dancers use for a number of exercises at the start of their practice.

Batterie: A succession of dance movements in which the feet are beaten together.

Explained below are a few of the terms that are found in the language of ballet. You will find that some of the explanations give a fuller account of words used in the main part of this book. However, we have also included some additional words which most young ballet-lovers will eventually hear, or read, and will want to know their meaning.

Corps de ballet: The members of a company who usually dance as a group, just as a chorus sing together.

Danseur noble: A male dancer with a noble classical style such as Anthony Dowell's.

Decor: The scenery of a ballet. The word can also include the costumes.

Divertissement: A group of show-piece dances which have little or no relation to a ballet's story, the most famous being in the last act of *The Sleeping Beauty*. Nowadays it can also mean a ballet without a story or a mood.

Elevation: The dancer's ability to leap in the air.

Enchaînement: A series of linked steps forming a continuous movement.

Entrechat: A jump in which a dancer's feet criss-cross in the air up to eight times, though the great Nijinsky is said to have performed an *entrechat* ten times!

Glissade: A sliding step in any direction.

Jete: A jump from one foot to the other. During the jump the foot on which the dancer will land is kicked forwards, sideways or backwards.

Line: The appearance of the body when the dancer is dancing or standing still. This all-important outline is partly a matter of training but also luck at birth. As everyone knows, the physique of a dancer has to be excellent.

The Ballet Master or Mistress: The person who is in charge of training the company's dancers and rehearsing the works that are being performed. It is his, or her, job to keep up the standard of a ballet after the choreographer has finished. He continues the choreographer's work and helps the dancers in their roles.

Movements in dancing: There are seven that students learn. These are: 1 *plier*, to bend; 2 *etendre*, to stretch; 3 *relever*, to rise; 4 *sauter*, to jump; 5 *elancer*, to dart; 6 *glisser*, to glide; 7 *tourner*, to turn.

Pas de deux: A dance for two dancers.

Pirouette: A turn on one leg with the dancer spinning round on one foot.

Pointe: The extreme tip of the toe. There are also *a trois quarts* (on the flexed toes); *a demi* (on the ball of the foot); and *a quart* (on the full ball of the foot with hardly raised heels).

Port de bras: It means literally, the carriage of the arms. Also, it is the name of a number of exercises developed to make sure that a dancer's arms are seen to best advantage. The positions are taught just as the five positions of the feet are taught.

Prima ballerina: The leading female dancer of a ballet company. There is also prima ballerina assoluta, a title that is very rarely used. Only two Russian dancers were awarded the title in 200 years!

Repertory: The works being performed by a company over a certain period or a season.

Terre à terre: Meaning ground to ground, its ballet meaning is a dance with not many jumps, though not necessarily a simple dance.

Tombé: When a dancer falls from one leg to the other, or falls from both feet to one, bending the knee on landing.

Tour en l'air: A turn in the air. There can also be double and occasionally triple turns. These spectacular feats are usually only performed by male dancers.

Tutu: The standard ballet skirt, made of nylon or tarlatan. It has been in use since Taglioni's day, when it was halfway between knee and ankle.

Working leg: The leg that performs a movement while the body's weight is being taken by the supporting leg.

Index

Bold face indicates pages on which illustrations appear.

★ ★